UNIT B



# WOODS

## Animals and Plants

## Contents

# The Apartment House Tree

*by Bette Killion*

In a plump, tall tree
at the edge of the woods,
many families live hidden away.

On the first floor,
a bushy–tailed squirrel and his wife
crack nuts with their sharp, pointed teeth.

Around the corner,
a prickly porcupine finds a vacant apartment
and decides she and her baby
will move right in.

In the basement,
the mole has tunneled
quiet, dark rooms among the roots.

High on the tree trunk,
a red–headed woodpecker is busy
with his long, sturdy beak,
carving a room of his own.

Upstairs,
snuggled into its nest on a leafy branch,
lives a family of hummingbirds.

Higher still, in a small, round hole,
the ruffle–feathered owl is tucked away,
sleeping the day through.

An orange and green tree frog
clasps his long toes around a branch,
his sleepy eyes blinking.

Under the humped, rough bark,
beetle and aphid families creep.

On the backs of leaves,
there are cocoon beds,
and butterflies just coming
out of their cocoons.

A skink
clings to his branch home
with five sticky, padded toes.

High up, inside the trunk of the tree,
is the home of the sly, masked, ring–tailed raccoons.

And in the very tip top
of the grand, tall hideaway
apartment house tree,
there is a place
just for me.

# Animals on Alert

Some animals use their body coverings to help them stay safe. Color and body markings can help to camouflage an animal. Other animals use sharp horns, quills, stingers, or hard shells to protect themselves.

This walking stick looks like a twig.

The turtle's hard shell is like armor.

A porcupine's sharp quills keep it safe.

Some animals use their body coverings to warn enemies.

This butterfly's bright colors warn attackers of its bad taste.

Many animals also use their wings or their legs to carry them away from danger.

A blue jay's wings carry it away.

## Show How Animals Protect Themselves

### You will need

paper strip

art supplies

Activity
Journal
10

animal sheet

1. Color and cut out the animals on the sheet.
2. Put the animals in order by size from smallest to largest. Then paste them in order on a strip of paper.
3. Discuss how the animals might protect themselves.
4. Choose one of the animals. Act out how it protects itself.

# Animals in Winter

Some animals grow warm coats to protect themselves from cold weather. Some birds fly south to warmer places. Other birds fluff their feathers to keep themselves warm and dry. A few animals sleep through the cold winter months.

The squirrel's fur keeps it warm.

The beaver makes its house ready for winter.

These birds fly south for winter.

This chickadee tries to stay warm.

How much does an animal's covering help keep it warm?

## Warm Winter Coats

### You will need

plastic jars

hot water

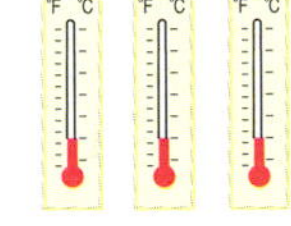
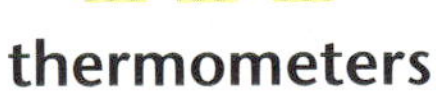
thermometers

feathers

wool scarf

recording sheet

1. **Hot** Label the jars 1, 2, and 3. Watch as your teacher puts hot water into each jar.

2. Use thermometers to measure the water temperature of each jar. Record the temperatures.

3. Place the jars outside. Tape feathers around Jar 1. Wrap a wool scarf around Jar 2. Leave Jar 3 bare.

4. Predict which jars will hold their heat.

5. Wait 10 minutes, then measure and record the water temperature. Repeat this two more times.

# What's for Lunch?

Some animals eat only meat. These animals are called meat eaters, or carnivores.

Frogs and snakes are a hawk's food.

Snakes eat mice and chipmunks.

A weasel eats mice, squirrels, and other small animals.

Some animals eat only plants. These animals are called plant eaters, or herbivores.

Deer graze on twigs and buds.

Chipmunks hunt for nuts and seeds.

Bark and twigs are a porcupine's favorite food.

Animals that eat both meat and plants are called omnivores. You belong in this group.

A mole feeds on worms and seeds.

Raccoons eat plants, meat, and fruits.

Insects, small animals, fruit, and eggs are a skunk's food.

# Woods Cafe

## You will need

crayons

large sheet of paper

1. Choose a woods animal.
2. Work with others who eat the same kinds of food. Make a menu.
3. Pretend you are the animal. Order a meal from the menu.

# Where Animals Live

The woods and the desert are both habitats for living things. Different animals live in each place.

garter snake

raccoon

deer

The weather in the woods may be warm in summer and cold in winter. Rain and snow often fall. Animals such as these find the food and shelter they need to stay alive.

spotted skunk

desert tortoise

Gila monster

The weather in the desert is hot and dry in summer. Rain hardly ever falls. Animals such as these find the food and shelter they need to stay alive.

jack rabbit

# Making an Animal

## You will need

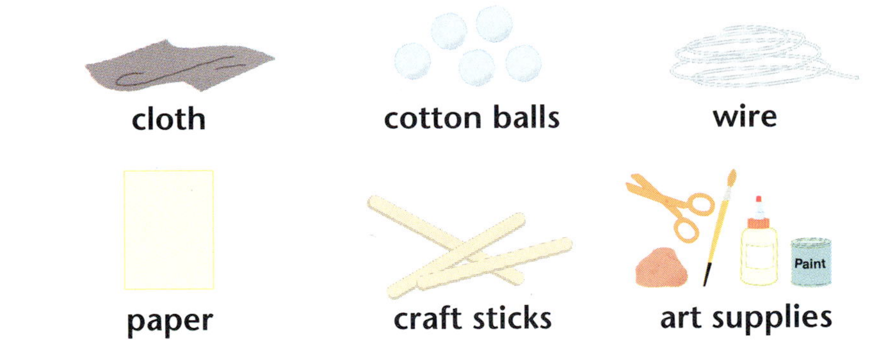


1. Think about the animal you will make.
   - Where does it live?
   - What does it need to live there?
   - What does it eat?
   - How does it protect itself?

2. Draw pictures of your animal. Show its home, what it eats, and how it protects itself.

3. Choose materials to make your animal.

4. Draw a habitat for your animal. Make a display. Then share your animal.

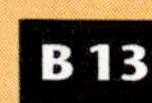

# Plant Protection

Many plants have coverings that protect them from animals and insects. Bark protects a tree. Some plants have fine hair on their leaves. Other plants have thorns or spines.

Bark covers the soft parts of this maple tree.

The hairs help protect the leaves from insects.

These holly leaves have sharp spines.

Some plants have poison in their sap. Still other plants taste or smell bad.

Poison ivy can cause an itchy rash.

Insects dislike the smell of marigolds.

# Make a Plant Mobile

## You will need

art supplies

hanger

toothpicks

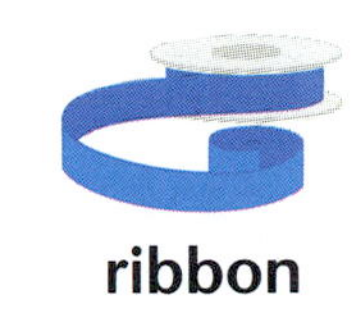

ribbon

paper plate

pipe cleaners

1. Choose one way plants protect themselves.
2. On one side of the plate, create a plant that protects itself this way.
3. Write about the plant's defenses on the other side of the plate.
4. Work with a group to make a mobile using ribbon and a hanger.

# Making Food

You know that animals eat to get the food they need. Green plants are different. Plants make their own food in their leaves.

To make food, leaves need three things:

- •water
- •light
- •air

Sunlight hits the green leaves. The leaves use the sunlight to change carbon dioxide and water into food.

Air goes in through tiny holes on the bottom of each leaf.

The roots and stem carry water to the leaves.

What happens if a plant doesn't get enough light?

# In Search of Light

## You will need

shoe box with lid

scissors

cardboard

bean plant

recording sheet

1. Use cardboard to make two walls with openings. Put the walls in the box. Cut a hole in one end of the box.
2. Put the plant in the end of the box that has no hole. On your paper, draw what it looks like. Put on the lid. Put the box on a sunny windowsill. Keep the plant damp.
3. Wait a week. Then take off the lid. On your paper, draw what you see.
4. Talk about what happened.

# Seeds on the Move

Most plants make many seeds. These seeds must leave the parent plant before they can grow. Seeds have different ways of moving.

**Wind** Some seeds travel by wind. Their parachute or wing shapes help them glide or float.

**Shooters** Some plants pop their seeds, shooting them away from the parent plant. This happens when the seed pod dries out.

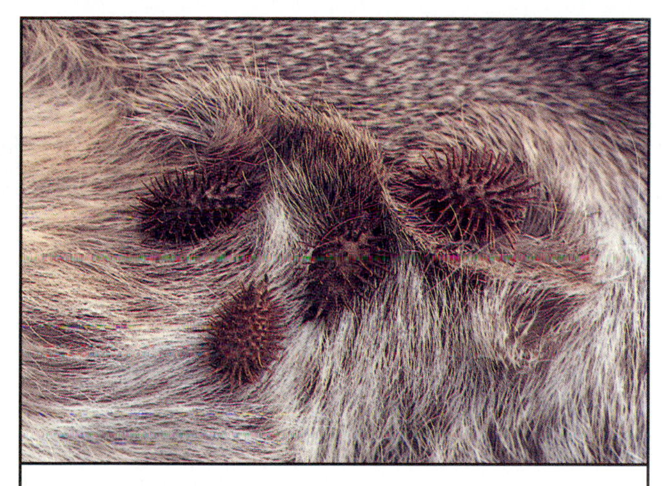

**Hitchhikers** Some seeds hitch a ride on people or animals. They have sharp hooks that grab hair or fur.

**Water** A few seeds travel long distances by water. These seeds have a waterproof husk to keep them dry.

# How Seeds Travel

## You will need

seeds

hand lens

water

clean sock

Activity Journal 16

recording sheet

1. Use a hand lens to look at the seeds.
2. Blow to see which seeds travel with the wind. Draw them on your paper.
3. Find out which seeds can float. Draw them.
4. Find out which seeds can hitchhike on fur or clothing. Draw them.

# Where Plants Live

The woods and the desert are both habitats for living things. Different plants live in each place.

grape hyacinth

Dutchman's-breeches

In many woods, warm, rainy summers and cool, snowy winters are usual. Tall trees and many types of plants grow well here. In autumn, leaves fall from trees and in spring appear again.

white oak

prickly pear

Desert weather is hot and dry. Fewer plants grow here. Desert plants often have thick leaves that store water. Sharp thorns protect some plants from animals.

organ-pipe cactus

# Make a Woodland Diorama

## You will need

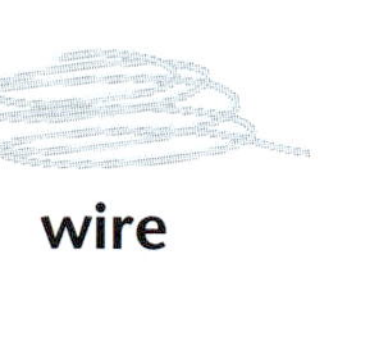

wire

art supplies

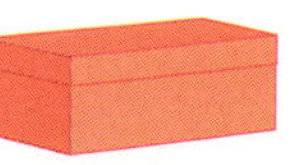

shoe box

cotton balls

gravel, dirt, or sand

plant parts

1. Think about the habitat you will make. What plants and trees grow there? What animals live there?
2. Plan your diorama. Turn the box on its side. Draw the habitat on the sides and back of the box.
3. Choose materials. Make trees and bushes. Add plants, leaves, dirt, and stones.
4. Make animals for your habitat. Place them where they live.
5. Make a card for your diorama. Tell about the plants and animals in your habitat.

# Meet a Naturalist!

Hi! I'm Lisa Lopez. I work as a naturalist at a nature center. I have spent a long time studying plants, animals, and other things in nature. Now I help other people understand what they see in nature. I also help them understand that animals and plants must have safe places to live.

Lisa Lopez

YOU CAN HELP

Sometimes people harm the environment in ways that make it harder for animals and plants to survive. One of the things that naturalists do to find out if the environment has changed is to keep track of the number of birds. Birds are counted each year at the same time and place. Fewer birds may mean that the environment has been harmed.

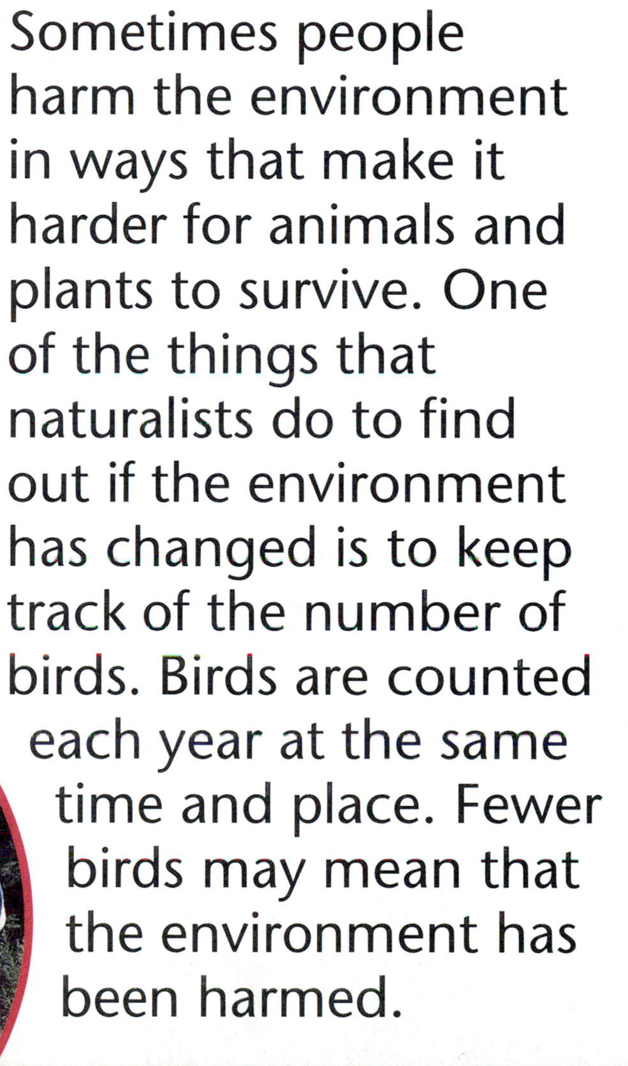

# Glossary

**bark** *page B14*
The outside covering of trees.

**body covering** *page B6*
The outside part of an animal, such as feathers, fur, scales, or shells.

**camouflage** *page B6*
Markings, such as stripes or spots, and colors on an animal's body that make it hard to see.

**carbon dioxide** *page B16*
A gas in the air that animals breathe out and plants take in and use to make food.

**carnivore** *page B10*
An animal that eats meat.

**desert** *page B12*
A dry area of land with few plants or animals.

**habitat** *page B13*
The place where a plant or animal naturally grows or lives.

**herbivore** *page B10*
An animal that eats plants.

**omnivore** *page B11*
An animal that eats both plants and animals.

**seed** *page B18*
The part of a plant that can grow into a new plant.